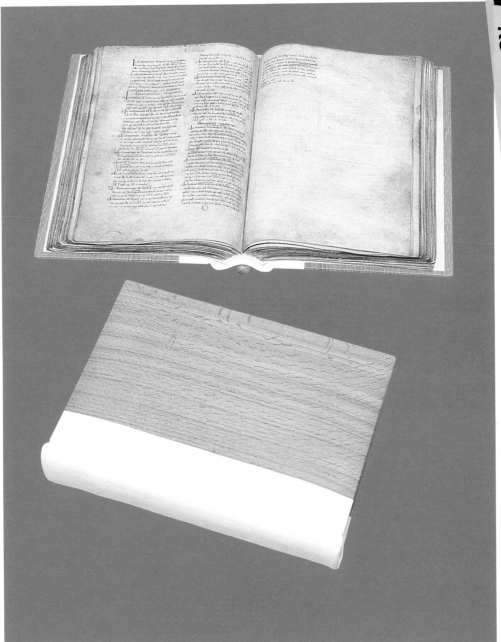

Two of the completed Domesday volumes, 1986.

Domesday Preserved

Helen Forde

London   HER MAJESTY'S STATIONERY OFFICE

© *Crown copyright 1986*
First published 1986

ISBN 0 11 440203 5

Printed for HMSO by Balding + Mansell Limited
Dd 738623 C60 8/86

Acknowledgements

This handbook could not have been written without the help of a great many people, in particular the two conservators, Frank Haynes and John Abbott, and the binder Don Gubbins who together made up the Domesday team.

Unpublished reports written for the Public Record Office by John Gowlett, Michael Gullick, Catherine Mortimer, Ron Reed and Ashok Roy have provided a basis for much of the text. Colleagues at the Public Record Office, in particular Elizabeth Hallam Smith, have been especially helpful. I should like to thank the Conservation Department and John Millen for their work on the photographs, and Peter Webb for his line drawings which are based on sketches done by Michael Gullick. Unless otherwise stated all the photographs are from the Public Record Office. The Eadwine psalter is reproduced by kind permission of the Master and Fellows of Trinity College Cambridge and Exon Domesday by kind permission of the Dean and Chapter of Exeter Cathedral. The gathering charts are reproduced with the kind permission of HMSO. I should also like to take the opportunity to thank the many people who have discussed the rebinding of Domesday Book and offered advice over the past two years. In particular, Roger Powell and Sandy Cockerell have spent much effort in helping us and Chris Clarkson of the Bodleian Library has been unstinting in his advice and encouragement: Michael Pascoe of Camberwell School of Art and Crafts assisted in the ink analysis, David Haddon Rees of the English Heritage discussed the age of the boards, and Simon Ferris, A E North and Clive Wainwright of the Victoria and Albert Museum considered the Domesday chest at length. The Conservation Department at the Public Record Office has borne the brunt of the Domesday activity, including those members not directly involved who have undertaken work for their colleagues and provided support. To them all and to others too numerous to mention I should like to extend my thanks.

Contents

Introduction   1

Materials and methods   9

Domesday bound and re-bound   25

Conservation and re-binding 1984-1986   33

Appendix A   Timetable of conservation and repair work
on Domesday Book 1984-1986   52
Appendix B   Radio-carbon data   53
Appendix C   Metal analysis   53

Index   55

LIST OF PLATES

Frontispiece. Two of the completed Domesday volumes, 1986.

COLOUR PLATES (pages 23-26)

A Eadwine Psalter. Trinity College Library, Cambridge. (MS R 17.1) f.283v.
B Little Domesday f.450r. Close up of colophon.
C Great Domesday, 'Tudor' covers, outer view.
D Abbreviatio (E 36/284)
E Completed volumes with carrying cases.

PLATES

Introduction
  1   Exon Domesday. Cathedral Library, Exeter.
  2   Domesday chest circa. 1500. German style iron bound chest in use for the storage of Domesday from about 1600.
  3   Farley's edition 1783.
  4   Photo-zincographic edition 1863. f.62v.

Materials and methods
  5   Great Domesday f.92r. Close up of folded corner showing amount of edge trimmed.
  6   Two methods of cutting sheets from skins.
  7   Gathering chart of Great Domesday. (pages 48 and 49)
  8   Great Domesday f.76r. Close up of half sheet inserted showing reruling.
  9   Little Domesday f.195r. Irregular sheet.
 10   Gathering chart of Little Domesday. (pages 50 and 51)
 11   Preparation for writing.
 12   Rulings.
 13   Ruling patterns.
 14   Great Domesday f.146r, 149v. Repaired.

15   Great Domesday f.313r. Close up of deletion.
16   Great Domesday f.63v. Script A and B.
17   Little Domesday f.450v. Close up of dry-point signatures, Henri D'Oilli and Sanson.

Domesday bound and rebound
18   Early sewing patterns.
19   Little Domesday, 'Tudor' covers, inside view.
20   Little Domesday, 'Tudor' covers, showing pin hole and remains of strap.
21   Metalwork on 'Tudor' boards.
22   Sir Francis Palgrave.
23   Little Domesday f.437v, 442r. Close up of Victorian repairer's name (J. Kew) in fold.
24   R. Riviere's bindings 1869. Great and Little Domesday.

Conservation and rebinding 1984-1986
25   Great Domesday. 1952 meeting guards.
26   Great Domesday. f.9v, 14r. Membrane badly creased.
27   1952 binding.
28   General view of conservation workshop.
29   Little Domesday, f.36r. 'Goldbeaters' skin on scored lines of text.
30   Little Domesday, f.387r. Centrefold distortion of parchment by excess moisture.
31   Oak boards for Great and Little Domesday, 1986.
32   Great Domesday. 1952 repair being damped for removal.
33   Paring centre repair piece.
34   Placing membrane into humidity cabinet.
35   Tensioning weights being placed into position.
36   Centre repair being placed into position.
37   Little Domesday. 'Goldbeaters' skin being applied to membrane at point of split.
38   Concertina guard of paper and herring bone sewing.
39   Text block before sewing of part 2 of Great Domesday.
40   Little Domesday. Pack sewing in the round on sewing frame.
41   Great Domesday. Head-bands partly sewn, back view.
42   Little Domesday. Rebates between drill holes being filed.
43   Little Domesday. Cords drawn on.

Introduction

The compilation of Domesday Book in 1086 was a feat unrivalled in contemporary Europe, although it is clear that the collection of information relating to estates and their value was not unknown to either the laity or the Church. Fiscal censuses had been conducted by the Romans, followed on the Continent by polyptychs and in England by geld rolls and hidage lists.[1] All preceded the Domesday inquisition, but none was on the same scale or apparently conducted as expeditiously. The majority were kept on rolls, unlike Domesday Book, but another example of a codex does survive in the polyptych of the Abbey of Prüm dating from 893. That is an ecclesiastical record, and it has been suggested that it was through the Church that Carolingian practices were transmitted across the Channel. At present there are no demonstrable links between such earlier records and the Domesday inquisition,[2] but the apparent efficiency with which the 1086 inquisition was carried out suggests that the collection of information in such a way was not new to the Anglo-Saxons.

The exact purpose of the inquisition was not recorded, but contemporaries were in little doubt that the prime object was the collection of taxes. A heavy geld had been levied during the previous year and the country faced the threat of invasion from Cnut, king of Denmark. In addition there was trouble in Scotland, France, Normandy and Anjou. Such unrest must have prompted the discussions which the Anglo-Saxon chronicle informs us took place at Gloucester in late 1085 and the order made by William to conduct an inquisition. William sent commissioners out to all the counties, excluding the lands north of the Tees and the middle Eden,

> and had them find out how many hundred hides there were in the shire, or what land and cattle the king himself had in the country, or what dues he ought to have in twelve months from the shire. Also, he had a record made of how much land his archbishops had, and his bishops and abbots and his earls ... and what or how much everybody had who was occupying land in England, in land and cattle, and how much money it was worth. So very narrowly did he have it investigated that there was no single hide nor a yard of land nor indeed ... one ox nor one cow nor one pig was there left out, and not put down in his record. And all these records were brought to him afterwards.[3]

Other chroniclers confirm the thorough manner in which the survey was carried out and Robert Losinga, bishop of Hereford, who was probably present at Gloucester when the arrangements were made, noted that

> other investigators followed the first: and men were sent into provinces which they did not know, and where they themselves were unknown in order that they might be given the opportunity of checking the first survey, and if necessary of denouncing its authors as guilty to the king.[4]

He added that the collection of royal taxes had provoked much violence, although whether because of the amounts demanded or the manner in which the demands were made is unspecified. The Anglo-Saxon chronicle noted that the king

acted according to his custom, that is to say he obtained a very great amount of money wherever he had any pretext for it whether just or unjust.[5]

William went to the Vexin in the summer of 1087, determined to wreak vengeance on his son, Robert Curthose, and the king of France, Philip I, who had begun devastating Normandy. He took a large force of mercenaries, themselves evidence that he had access to enough money to pay them, and was subsequently mortally injured during the sack of Mantes that autumn. It is not known whether he had seen any of the returns to the inquests before he left England at the end of 1086,[6] but his death meant, amongst other things, an end to the final recension of the findings of the various commissions. Almost immediately the information became obsolete for taxation purposes, although its value as a legal document against which there was no appeal had hardly begun. However, no such quantity of information had ever been brought together in that form before: it included details of land tenure, possessions, land use, the history of the changes forced upon the country as a result of the Norman conquest and an up-to-date assessment of the value of the conquered lands. To William it also underlined his vital role as the legitimate successor to Edward the Confessor and the related position of his tenants in chief.

The two volumes, already known as Domesday before 1180,[7] were brought together in the custody of the royal treasury in Winchester where they remained during the twelfth century until the Exchequer found them a more permanent home at Westminster. The larger volume, the final form of the results of the inquests, contains information about all the counties except the four northern ones, some towns such as London and Winchester, and the eastern part of the country covered by the smaller volume. Little Domesday contains what was meant to be the penultimate version of the text for the counties of Essex, Norfolk and Suffolk, and which may not have reached the scriptorium at Winchester in time to be assimilated to the rest. In consequence it was found to be convenient to keep the two volumes together. Other texts, such as that contained in the Exon Domesday, had already been incorporated into the main volume and it was therefore less important to keep them in the same place. The colophon at the end of Little Domesday must have been added shortly afterwards:

> In the year one thousand and eighty-six from the Incarnation of our Lord, and in the twentieth year of the reign of William there was made this survey, not only through these three counties, but also through others.[8]

The subsequent centuries witnessed the growing importance of the results of the inquest as binding evidence in matters of landholding and ancient demesne. Modern scholars still debate the usefulness of the information to the royal administration before the use of written records became more common, but the volumes were regarded sufficiently highly to warrant the production of copies in cartularies, extracts in legal records, and at least three comprehensive abbreviations,[9] by the thirteenth century. The medieval users of the book turned increasingly to the text to confirm lands and rights, although it was becoming of less importance as a feudal register or as a guide to landholders. It was used alike by those with considerable wealth and by those with few pretensions. In 1256 the king insisted, on the authority of Domesday Book, that the inhabitants of Chester should pay for the repair of a bridge in the town,[10] but it was also by reference to Domesday that the ancient demesne tenants of Godmanchester upheld their status and freedom from paying tolls for at least three centuries.[11] Increasingly, too, the volumes began to be used for antiquarian and historical purposes, while still supplying the authority for legal decisions.

Antiquarian interest and appreciation were not confined to those involved in writing chronicles or histories, but included the deputy chamberlains who had custody of the volumes in the Receipt of the Exchequer and were charged with the duty of making searches and copying extracts. Arthur Agarde, who was a deputy chamberlain from 1575 to 1615, promoted much of that interest, but from the late fifteenth century the deputy chamberlains had adopted a facsimile script for the authenticated copies which the Exchequer sold. By the early seventeenth century the text was beginning to be cited in dissertations on land holding, on ancient demesne, on parish histories, on measurements of land, and on place-names. Later in that century the theme of the 'Norman yoke' was widely canvassed and the arguments over the origins of the constitution raged hotly, Whigs and Tories adopting different views and interpretations of the evidence provided by Domesday Book.

Their polemics preceded a serious study of the Anglo-Saxons in the eighteenth century which relied more heavily on original documents

2   *Domesday chest circa. 1500.*
German style iron bound chest in use
for the storage of Domesday from
about 1600.

Ibi . 1 . hida geld . Tra . ē . 11 . car . In dn̄io . ē dimid car . 7 1 . feruus .
7 pbr 7 11 . uilli 7 1 . bord cū . 1 . car . 7 molin feruie\s aulæ .
Ibi . 1 . ac̄ p̄ti 7 dimid .   T.R.E . ualb . v1 . fol . Modo . v111 . fol .
Ifd̄ . W . ten WITELEI . 7 Pagen 7 Odard de eo . Leuenot tenuit
ut lib hō . Ibi . 11 . hidæ geld . Tra . ē . 11 . car . In dn̄io . ē una cū . 1 .
feruo . Ibi . 1 . ac̄ p̄ti . Silua . 1 . leuu lḡ . 7 dimid lat̄ . Val . v1 . fol .
Ifd̄ . W . ten GOSTREL . 7 Radulf de eo . Colben tenuit ut lib hō .   IN MILDESTVICH HD
Ibi . 1 . uirg geld . Tra . ē . 11 . boū . Wafta fuit 7 eft . IN HAMSTAN HD .
Wills ten de comite ALDREDELIC . Brun tenuit 7 lib hō fuit .
Ibi . 1 . hida geld . Tra . ē . 1111 . car . Wafta fuit 7 eft . Silua . 11 . leuu lḡ .
7 11 . lat̄ .   IN MILDESTVIC HVND . ⌐ T.R.E . ualb . xx . fol .
Wills ten de com LECE . Haften tenuit 7 lib hō fuit .
Ibi dimid hida geld . Tra . ē . 1 . car . Wafta fuit 7 eft .

3   *Farley's edition 1783.*

4 Photo-zincographic edition 1863. f.62v.

and less on interpretation. Extracts from Domesday continued to be made in local histories, but increasing concern was expressed over the accuracy of some of them. A feeling therefore arose that Domesday should be published in full. Suggestions were also made, first to the Society of Antiquaries in a paper by Philip Carteret Webb in December 1755, that publication would mitigate any catastrophe that might befall the volumes which were then kept in the Chapter House at Westminster. In 1767 Parliament gave its consent to the project, and in 1783 Abraham Farley's facsimile-type edition was finally published.

The use of the originals seems to have declined as a result of the publication and it may have been for that reason that the fact that the boards of the larger volume had been attacked by worm was unremarked until John Caley reported it to the Record Commissioners in 1819. As a result both volumes were rebound, although not in a style

5

that pleased Sir Francis Palgrave, later to become the first deputy keeper of the public records. Further texts and indexes related to Domesday were published during the early years of the nineteenth century by the Record Commission. Their availability probably increased public interest in a proposal put forward in 1861 by Sir Henry James, the director of the Ordnance Survey, that the text of one county, Cornwall, should be copied as an experiment by the photo-zinco-graphic method which had been developed in his department. By that time Domesday Book was housed in the new Public Record Office in Chancery Lane, where it was taken from the Chapter House in 1859. That first exercise in making the text available for palaeographical studies without recourse to the original was highly successful, and Cornwall was succeeded by other counties. The volumes were dis-mantled, taken to Southampton and photographed in the open air, watched over by an assistant keeper from the Record Office, William Basevi Saunders. By 1864 they were back in London and a debate began over their future role. In the 1850s the Public Record Office had been in favour of displaying them to the public, but their history as museum pieces did not begin until a controversy over their rebinding, with an attendant emphasis on the best method of display, had been resolved. Suitable premises were needed within the Office, an amenity not avail-able until after the 1886 Domesday celebrations which were organised by the Royal Historical Society and included a meeting addressed by Hubert Hall, one of the assistant keepers, from the balcony of the Round Room in the Public Record Office.

The celebration also included some major contributions by J H Round, who was to dominate Domesday studies for many years. His interest was followed by others, notably by F W Maitland, and with the existence of the facsimile copies the debate over the text continued unimpeded by the need to consult the original. In the early 1890s the volumes were put on display in a room above the gate in the new facade of the Record Office built on Chancery Lane and when the new museum was opened in 1902, on the site of the Old Rolls Chapel, they were removed there and placed as its centre piece in a floor case. Fears for the safety of the volumes led to their removal to Bodmin prison during the First World War when the threat of bombing became a reality, and to Shepton Mallet for the duration of the Second World War. Returned to London, they were again displayed in the fireproof cases which had been installed shortly before the outbreak of war. Increasing curiosity about the physical make-up of the two volumes, however, and a distaste for the Victorian binding which the deputy keeper, Sir Hilary Jenkinson, regarded as out of keeping with the contents, led to the first physical examination of them followed by the rebinding in 1952. The results were published in *Domesday Rebound* (HMSO, 1954) and added considerably to knowledge of the compilation of the text and the way in which the larger volume was written. Since then interest has not diminished, and the occasion of the nine hundredth anniversary has offered the opportunity for further investigation and study. Both volumes have been dismantled, conserved, and photographed before rebinding, to allow the publication of a full-colour facsimile.

REFERENCES

1   S Harvey, 'Domesday Book and its Predecessors', *English Historical Review* 86, (1971), pp.753-73.

2   J Percival, 'The Precursors of Domesday' in P H Sawyer, (ed.), *Domesday Book: a reassessment,* (Edward Arnold, 1985).

3   Anglo Saxon Chronicle E (1085). D C Douglas, (ed.), *English Historical Documents,* (Eyre and Spottiswoode, 1953).

4   W H Stevenson, (ed.), 'Chronicle of Marianus Scotus', *English Historical Review* 22, (1907), pp.72-84.

5   Anglo Saxon Chronicle E (1085).

6   R Welldon Finn, 'The Immediate Sources of the Exchequer Domesday', *Bulletin of the John Rylands Library* 40, (1957), pp.47-78.

7   For a discussion of the various terms used to describe the text see E M Hallam *Domesday Book Through Nine Centuries,* (Thames & Hudson, 1986), p.35.

8   E 31/1.

9   The Exchequer Abbreviatio (E 36/284), Domesday Breviate (E 164/1), British Library Arundel 153.

10   *Calendar of Liberate Rolls* IV, 282.

11   E M Hallam, *op. cit.,* p.50.

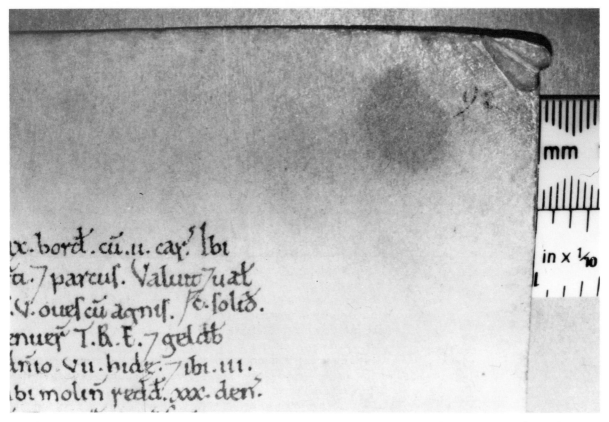

 x.borđ.cū.ıı.caỷ ĺbi
a.7 parcuĺ. Valuıȝʒuaĺ
N.oueĺcū agnıĺ. ẽ.folıd.
enueȝ T.Ŕ.Ē.7 gelđ̃
ãnto .vıı.hıdȝ.7ıbı.ııı.
ıbı molıñ ređđ.xxx.deñ.

5 *Great Domesday f.92r. Close up of folded corner showing amount of edge trimmed.*

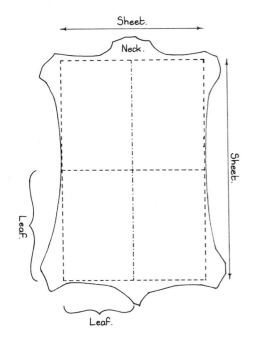

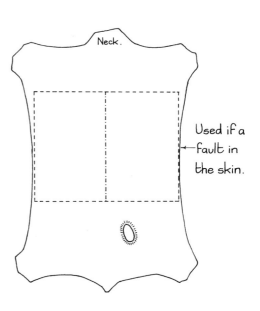

6 *Two methods of cutting sheets from skins.*

Materials and methods

Both volumes consist of parchment leaves made from sheepskins, although the geographical areas from which they were taken are likely to have been different.

Great Domesday was almost certainly written in Winchester where local sheep would have supplied the needs of the chancery. Most of the 383 folios were originally the full width of the sheepskin, approximately $20'' \times 14\frac{1}{2}''$, although the present size is smaller. A folded corner on folio 92 shows that at least $\frac{1}{4}''$ has been trimmed off. The original size was similar to that most commonly used in monastic libraries for a long text.[1] In every case the membrane was folded and sewn down the centre, which corresponded to the spine of the animal: the resulting size of the pages indicates that the sheep were small by modern standards. The plan appears to have assigned a complete gathering (of four folded membranes) or gatherings to each county, except for six in which the county headings fall in the middle of a gathering. The standard was not adhered to rigidly, and was applied to only 21 gatherings of the total of 47. Extra double and a few single folios appear to have been added where necessary. Half-sheets and used parchment which had previously been ruled the other way were occasionally inserted.[2] Uncertainty about the total quantity of information to be included made such variations necessary: some of the gaps left by the scribe indicate that he did not always have all the information to hand before starting a section.

Little Domesday is composed of a larger number of smaller sheets of parchment, fewer of which show signs of having been cut from the underbelly or groin of the animal. It originally comprised 451 folios, each sheet measuring about $22''$ across the full width of the bi-folium, and $8''$ in length. In feel the sheets are less pliable than those of Great Domesday and do not appear to have been pared down substantially, or abraded to the same extent in preparation for writing. There is no sign that they have been trimmed, and most of the fore-edges still have the prick-marks that guided the ruling. The gatherings are more uniformly composed of four double, folded sheets of parchment (48 out of an original total of 56) with fewer inserted sheets. The contents of the volume, a more detailed account than would probably have been incorporated into the large volume had the whole operation not been brought to a halt, required several gatherings for each county, and the scribes seem to have been supplied with enough information to avoid leaving spaces. Whether the sheep were from the three counties, Essex, Suffolk, and Norfolk, it is impossible to tell, but all the grain patterns are similar.

The method of preparation of the parchment would have been the same wherever the skins originated. They all came from mature animals and had a high fat content. Once selected, they would have been washed by the parchmenter and then placed in a lime-pit to loosen the hairs and remove the fatty layers. Finally they would be stretched on a frame and dried flat under tension, while being scraped and pumiced to remove further fat. Failure to remove all the fat at that stage has caused natural tanning to continue during the centuries, because many of the molecules of fat in sheepskins are readily oxidised to form complex aldehydes and epoxide polymers, both of which have tanning action. In addition, the collagen fibres of sheepskin parchment cross-link at ordinary temperatures, or on exposure to sunlight, to yield a weak kind

8 *Great Domesday f.76r. Close up of half sheet inserted showing reruling.*

9 *Little Domesday f.195r. Irregular sheet.*

of leather known as oil-tanned stock. Development of its characteristic yellow colour, smoothness, flexibility and water repellency is due to the oxidation products of the liquid fats which have marked filling and lubricative qualities. The natural oil on human hands deposited in the frequent handling of the volumes has increased those tendencies. Thus the colour of the membranes of Great Domesday is noticeably yellower than that of Little Domesday which has been less used and is less pliable.[3]

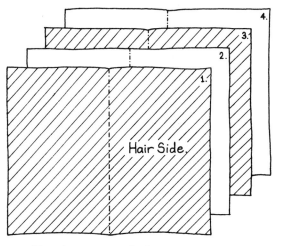

Hair Side.

Sheets assembled into quires.

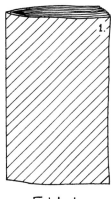

Folded.

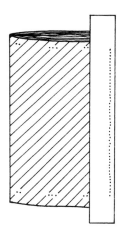

Pricked head & tail. Template laid on to prick down foredge.

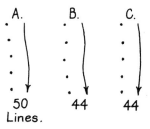

A.   B.   C.

50   44   44
Lines.

A constant relationship in the first few holes in the quires imply the use of a template.

Before the scribe started writing, the skins had to be cut to size and arranged in groups of four to form gatherings. To avoid variations in colour, flesh side would be placed to flesh side (the inner surface of the skin) and hair side (the outer surface) to hair side. Such volumes were usually arranged so that they began and ended with a hair side. The sheets would then be folded and pricked right through with a sharp knife or an awl. A template was used on Great Domesday for the holes at the fore-edge and the evidence of at least three still remains.[4]

The gathering was then disassembled and each sheet ruled with a point, probably of bone or metal, using a straight edge to make a regular series of horizontal and vertical lines on the hair side, the pricking acting as a guide. It has been estimated that each bi-folium would take at least 15 minutes to prepare in that way. At first the scribe used 44 lines to the page on Great Domesday, but later there are up to 53 and on occasion the lines ruled were subsequently ignored. It seems likely that more than one quire was ruled at the same time. The vertical arrangement is also variable, in particular the head of the columns is rarely the same width as the gap at the tail. That is true of the whole of Great Domesday and suggests the work of one hand. In Little Domesday, where the writing was carried out by a number of different scribes, each probably did his own ruling to some plan, albeit much simpler than that for the large volume. The number of lines to the page varies, but is most commonly 23 or 24, and the work was written in a single format.[5]

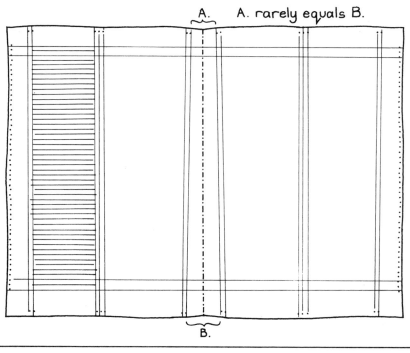

A. A. rarely equals B.

B.

Ruler long enough to extend width of sheet.

12 Rulings.

Earliest Ruling Pattern.

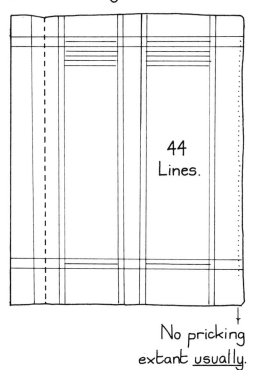

44
Lines.

No pricking
extant _usually_.

Middle Ruling Pattern.

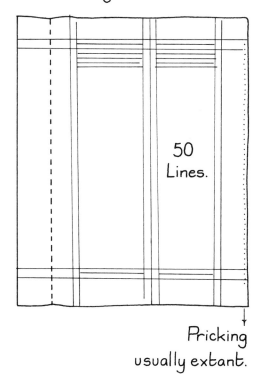

50
Lines.

Pricking
usually extant.

Late Ruling Pattern.

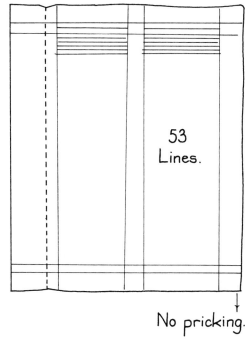

53
Lines.

No pricking.

Last Ruling Pattern.

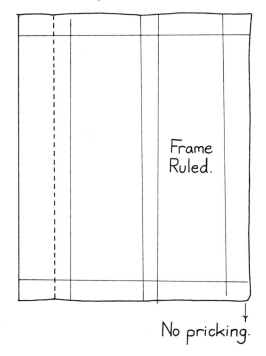

Frame
Ruled.

No pricking.

13   Ruling patterns.

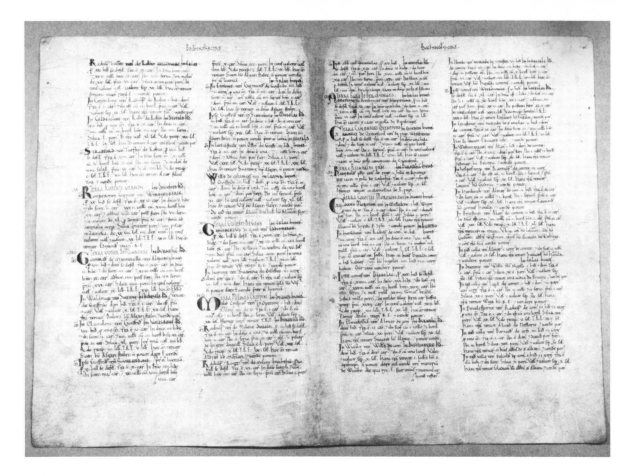

14 Great Domesday f.146r, 149v. Repaired.

The two-column format adopted for Great Domesday was rare in England before the Conquest, but was adopted in monastic scriptoria for larger works towards the end of the eleventh century. In planning the lay-out the scribe seems to have chosen a slightly larger writing area than was usual in monastic books, although that may be due to the utilitarian nature of the text and the lack of need for ornate embellishment. A similar ratio (1:2) was adopted for the relationship of minim height to interlinear height as that found in monastic volumes of comparable size, although when circumstances demanded greater compression that ideal was abandoned. The running headings of the names of the counties was unusual, being a device sometimes used earlier but not reintroduced in other books until the second quarter of the twelfth century. The need for easy reference may have dictated its use and it appears that the rubrication in Little Domesday was probably added after the text had been compiled. It is tempting to see it as a preliminary to the first binding, shortly after completion of the text, when it was clear that the information was not to be assimilated into the larger volume.

The text is likely to have been written with a pen made from the primary feathers of birds' wings, hardened either by age or merely from continuous use with ferro-gallo-tannate ink (see colour plate A). The point was probably sharpened with a knife as the writing continued. The knife would also be used to hold the parchment down on the

14

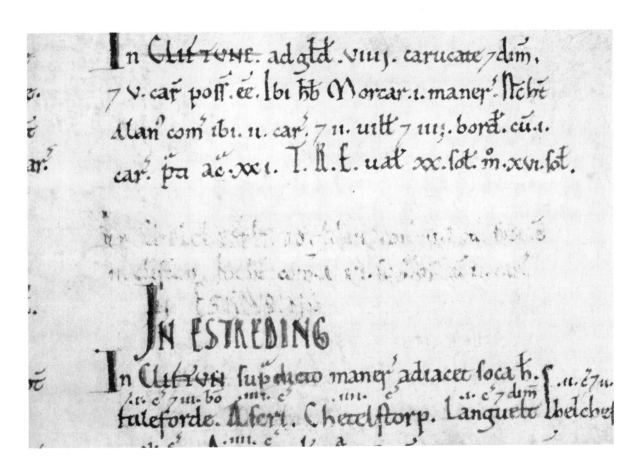

In CLIFTONE. ad gld .viiij. carucate 7 dim.
7 v. car poſſ. ee. Ibi hb Morzar .i. maneŕ. Stcht
Alan' com' ibi. ii. car' 7 ii. uilt 7 iiij. bord. cu .i.
car'. pa ac .xxi. T. R. E. ual xx. ſot. m. xvi. ſot.

JN ESTREDING

In CLIFTUN ſup dicto maneŕ adiacet ſoca h. ſ. .ii. c' 7 ii.
tuleforde. Aſert. Chetelſtorp. Languet Lbetchet

15 Great Domesday f.313r. Close up of deletion.

sloping surface of the desk (which was used by the scribe in order to control the flow of ink) and to scrape the parchment if a word had to be erased.[6]

Ferro-gallo-tannate ink was in common use at the time. Made up from a solution of galls, gum arabic and ferrous sulphate, it may have had colour added such as carbon, or it may have been left to oxidise, when it would turn black within a matter of days. The brown colour of much of the writing today is due to change over time, but variation within it makes it possible to see where the scribe was supplied with a new supply of ink.[7] Both volumes display the same characteristics in the black ink used for the text, but the reds are different. The bright red used for the running titles, chapter titles, chapter numbers, large initials, initial letters to subparagraphs, and the through-lining (equivalent to underlining) of certain words in Great Domesday is vermilion (red mercuric sulphide). Microscopic analysis also revealed particles of pigment which might be natural cinnabar or an artificial form which is indistinguishable at present from the natural matter. In Little Domesday, however, the pigment in the more orange-coloured red is red lead, probably prepared by roasting lead white in air; a few traces were still present in the sample analysed.

Results of the microscopic investigation of both reds were confirmed by x-ray diffraction analysis.[8] Difference in the medium used is not particularly surprising since both were in common use at the time. However, the use of the same medium for the colophon (see colour plate B), running titles, chapter numbers, and some of the chapter titles in Little Domesday suggests that they were written at the same time, after 1086 but before the second binding, because the pin then placed on the back board has rusted through the middle of one of two dry-point names on the back of the sheet on which the colophon is written.

The method of working adopted by the Domesday scribe, the length of time the work took, and his identity are matters for speculation. The greater part of Great Domesday is in the hand of a single scribe, although there is evidence of a second writer[9] who was also reading the text and making corrections. Such a pattern was not uncommon in monastic scriptoria. The use of two men strongly suggests that they were working from exemplars, since the task of editing the information being returned from the circuits was formidable. That, again, was common practice in monastic scriptoria, some exemplars of such texts having survived to be copied in their turn.[10] The fact that none has survived from the Winchester scriptorium has led to doubts about their existence, but against that it must be remembered that a great deal of the other contemporary material presumed to have existed has also disappeared.

The time taken to complete the work also suggests more than one scribe, even if only one did the writing. Calculations by modern calligraphers[11] suggest that six columns a day would have been about the most a scribe might expect to accomplish; that is similar to, although possibly a little less than, contemporary eleventh-century estimates of 250-280 lines a day. There is no doubt that Domesday was written very speedily, but the idea that the work could have been completed within 240 days, before William's departure to Normandy at the end of 1086,[12] seems unrealistic, and it may be that the account in the Peterborough chronicle relating that 'all the writings' were brought to William before his departure to Normandy refers not to the completed text of Great Domesday but to the circuit returns, including Little Domesday.[13] It is generally accepted that the work stopped when William died at Mantes on 9 September 1087, which might therefore have allowed a further nine months' work on the compilation of the larger volume. Recent discoveries about the first binding (see p.X) confirm that the membranes were probably bound up shortly after their partial completion, after William Rufus's accession.

The identity of the scribe remains a mystery which has teased successive Domesday scholars. Comparison between Exon Domesday, one of the satellites still surviving, and the entries in Great Domesday led V H Galbraith to suggest that Samson, named in two entries[14] and known to have been chaplain to both William I and William II and later bishop of Worcester, was the scribe.[15] The distinctiveness of the style of the main scribe of Great Domesday lies in its qualities as a book hand, a version of Caroline miniscule, widely used by contemporaries in northern Europe. It has a tendency to roundness even when compressed, and is noticeably different from the more pointed, pure Norman book hand used by the second scribe. That hand appears to be that which corrected Great Domesday and appended additional information, and is possibly that of a superior to the main scribe whose hand clearly dominates the text. Samson was an influential man and it has also been suggested that he had connections with the circuit which covered Essex, Norfolk, and Suffolk.[16] Lanfranc, Archibishop of Canterbury,

16 Great Domesday f.63v. Script A and B.

wrote to an unknown correspondent, addressed merely as 'S', about lands pertaining to the archbishop in the area covered.[17] Identification of 'S' with Samson must remain speculative, but the decipherment of the second name written with a broad stylus in dry point on the verso of the page on which the colophon is written in Little Domesday has added to the body of evidence. The first name is Henri D'Oilli and has been known for some time, although his connexion with the volume is obscure. The second name, however, has now been read as Sanson, a form of the name which would have been perfectly acceptable to contemporaries. The purpose of the stylus-drawn letters is as difficult to determine as the date at which they were added, but on the assumption that they were contemporary, and they must precede the late Romanesque binding which placed a pin on the back board (see p. X), the evidence is tantalizing.

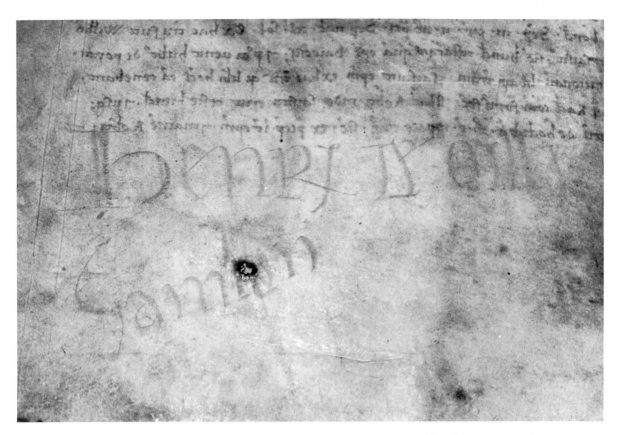

17 Little Domesday f.450v. Close up of dry-point signatures, Henri D'Oilli and Sanson.

REFERENCES

1   N Ker, *English Manuscripts in the century after the Norman Conquest* (Oxford University Press, 1960), p.41.

2   A Rumble, 'The palaeography of the Domesday manuscript', in P H Sawyer, (ed.), *Domesday Book: a re-assessment,* pp.33-57.

3   R Reed, unpublished report on the Domesday parchment undertaken for the Public Record Office, 1984.

4   M Gullick, unpublished report on the palaeography of Great Domesday undertaken for the Public Record Office, 1985.

5   *Ibid.*

6   Particularly E 31/2, f.G.

7   M Gullick, unpublished report.

8   Ashok Roy, National Gallery, unpublished report of microscopic and x-ray diffraction analysis of the red Domesday inks.

9   M Gullick, unpublished report, identifies one whole entry (63v), some additional entries (190r, 191v, 283r) and some other substantial passages as written by the second scribe.

10   N Ker, *op. cit.,* p.11.

11   The first calculation was done by A J Fairbank, *Domesday Rebound,* (HMSO 1954), p.34. It has been confirmed by M Gullick.

12   Anglo Saxon Chronicle E (1085).

13   R Weldon Finn, *Domesday Book: a guide,* (Phillimore, 1973), p.20

14   Liber Exoniensis, f.153r and Great Domesday, (E 31/2), f.87r.

15   V H Galbraith, 'Notes on the career of Samson, bishop of Worcester (1096-1112)' *English Historical Review* 82, (1967), pp.86-101.

16   F Barlow, 'Domesday Book: a letter of Lanfranc', *English Historical Review* 98, 1963, pp.284-9.

17   H Clover and M Gibson, (eds.), *The letters of Lanfranc ...,* (Oxford University Press, 1976), pp.170-171.

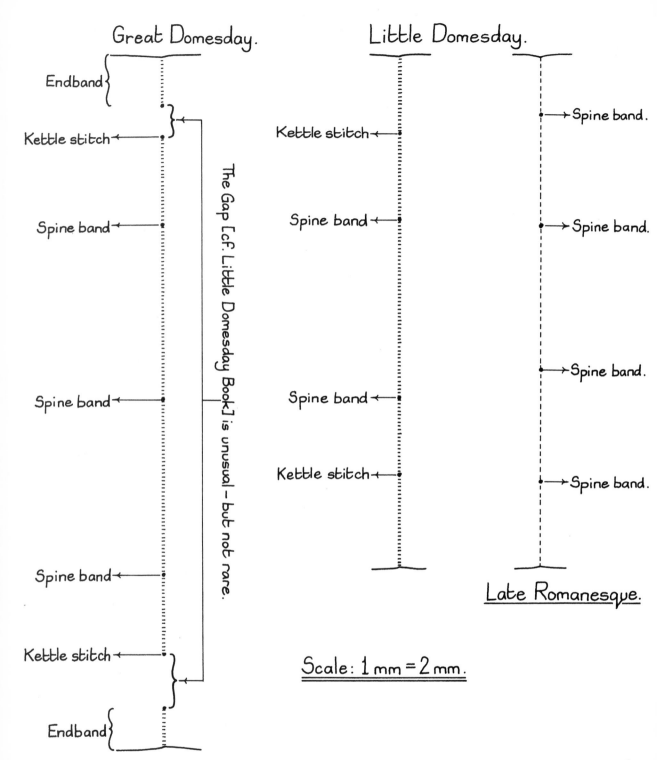

Great Domesday.

Endband

Kettle stitch ←

Spine band ←

Spine band ←

Spine band ←

Kettle stitch ←

Endband

The Gap [c.f. Little Domesday Book] is unusual – but not rare.

Little Domesday.

Kettle stitch ←

Spine band ←

Spine band ←

Kettle stitch ←

→ Spine band.

→ Spine band.

→ Spine band.

→ Spine band.

Late Romanesque.

Scale: 1 mm = 2 mm.

18   *Early sewing patterns.*

Domesday bound and re-bound

Conjectures about the compilation of the text and the identity of its scribe are matched by attempts to unravel the history of the binding of the two volumes. Until the nineteenth century there is no evidence other than the survival of the boards themselves to explain the decisions which must have been taken about the various bindings. Three sets of boards remain in the custody of the Public Record Office, the earliest being boards of varying date, covered with brown calf and decorated with metal bosses; the second are of heavily stamped black leather on card dating from 1869, and the third pair are those which were put on in 1952. From them and from the evidence of the parchment membranes, something of the early history of the binding of Domesday can be extracted.

The eleventh- and twelfth-century references that we have to the text are uninformative because the varied use of the words *carta, rotulus* and *liber* suggests that those terms did not then have the precise meanings which they have subsequently acquired. Nevertheless the manuscript was completed in its last two stages in book form, and evidence in the gutters of the bi-folia suggests that the first binding took place shortly after the text was completed. Prick holes near, but not in, the gutter, and through the quire indicate the stations for the three spine bands on which Great Domesday was originally bound, and the two for Little Domesday. The kettle-stitch stations are indicated in similar fashion and traces also remain of the endbands where slight blue staining has occurred on the parchment. In Great Domesday there is a sizeable gap between the kettle stitch and the endband, evidence which may serve to identify the particular binder or style of binding. The fact that the pattern was not repeated on Little Domesday supports the view that the two were probably not bound in the same place. Although it is not possible to date this binding, it must predate the late Romanesque binding for which we still have the boards of Little Domesday. The position of the four spine bands on which the latter was then bound do not correspond to the prick holes in the parchment.

Those boards, removed in 1819 and carefully kept, have been referred to as the 'Tudor' boards, since, like the boards for the larger volume, they are now covered in brown calf leather and decorated with metal bosses, Tudor in style. Despite the name, however, the research carried out in 1952 demonstrated that they were much older.[1] Made of oak, they bear evidence of late twelfth- or early thirteenth-century work with careful tunneling and chanelling characteristic of a late Romanesque style, not later than about 1225. Further evidence, now covered up, on the front board, is recorded in *Domesday Rebound*. Radio-carbon dating has confirmed that these boards have a mean date of about 1100 (see Appendix B).

The first written evidence of further work on the books appears in an Issue Roll: on 5 December, 14 Edward II (1320)[2] William le Bokbyndere of London was paid 3s 4d 'pro ligacione et de novo reparacione libri de Domesday in quo continentur Comitatus Essex, Norff' et Suff'' (for sewing and new repair of the Domesday Book which contains the counties of Essex, Norfolk, and Suffolk). Exchequer officials and their documents are known to have followed Edward II around the country and Domesday Book travelled to York the previous year.[3] That was not an isolated occasion and the binding of the smaller volume may have been damaged in transit. The remains of leather bands were discovered

19 *Little Domesday, 'Tudor' covers, inside view.*

20 *Little Domesday, 'Tudor' covers, showing pin hole and remains of strap.*

A Eadwine Psalter. Trinity College Library, Cambridge. (MS R 17.1) f.283v.

23

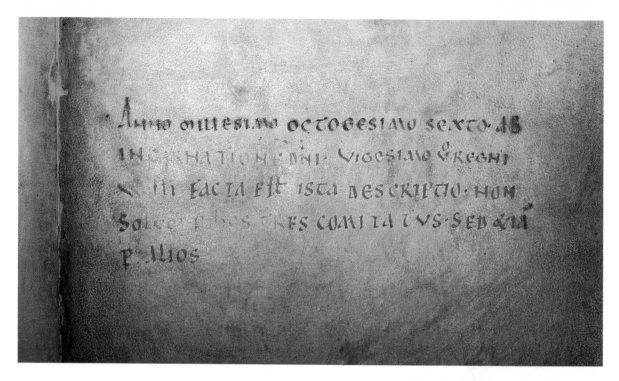

B Little Domesday f.450r. Close up of colophon.

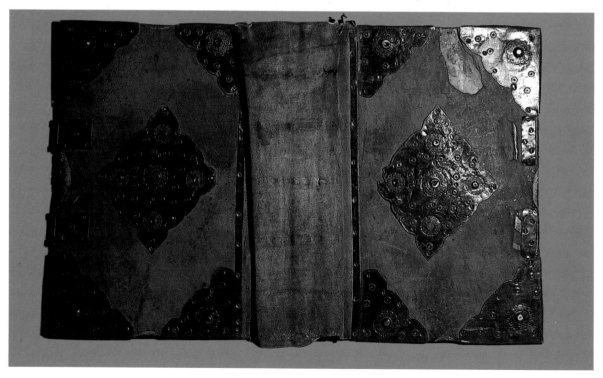

C Great Domesday, 'Tudor' covers, outer view.

24

D Abbreviatio (E 36/284)

E Completed volumes with carrying cases.

in 1952 in the holes in the front board, and the white alum-tawed skin turn-over stuck to the inner face of the back board has been given a fourteenth-century radio-carbon date. The remains of the strap, alum-tawed skin stained pink, were insufficient for dating in that way and speculation remains as to whether the strap together with the pin in the back board was a thirteenth- or fourteenth-century addition.

The date of the brown calf leather which covers both sets of boards is not distinctly determinable; that which covers the oak boards of Little Domesday has been given a mean radio-carbon date early in the fifteenth century while that of Great Domesday is nearly a century later. It is not impossible that the later covering over the beech boards, which were also new, was an attempt, at the later date, to match the earlier boards of Little Domesday. It also seems likely that the old boards of Great Domesday were too broken for further use by the sixteenth or early seventeenth century and were replaced, whilst those of Little Domesday, less used, were still regarded as serviceable.

Whatever the sequence of events, the metal bosses on both sets of boards were added at the same time, analysis of the metal having confirmed that they were made from a single sheet of brass, or from several sheets of very similar manufacture (see Appendix C). Made by the granulation technique which did not begin to be used in England until the 1570s, the bosses give a clear indication of a late Tudor or early Stuart interest in the volumes which it is tempting to connect with the deputy chamberlain Arthur Agarde (see colour plate C). The distinctive purity of the brass, in particular the absence of any lead and tin, suggests that they are more likely to be early Stuart in date. Visible repair work on the cover of the smaller volume consists of two types of metal, indicating two stages in repair. The first (Plate 21, items H-L) is of a lower purity brass than the decoration with a lower zinc content, although probably still made by granulation technique. The second type (M-N) reverts to a high purity with some lead and with over 33% metallic zinc, which indicates that it must be later than 1650, the earliest European date for the introduction of post-granulation techniques. Both types of metals in the repairs appear on both volumes, and from that date the history of the binding of the two volumes appears to run in parallel. Those results might be interpreted initially as an attempt to replace the function of the medieval pin with clasps, and subsequently to repair these on Great Domesday, and to repair the later split in the boards of Little Domesday.

During the eighteenth century the two volumes were stored in the Chapter House, still cared for by the deputy chamberlains whose activities are attested in the quantity of extracts they left behind them. A report by John Caley in 1819 to the Record Commissioners stated that worm had been found in the beech boards of Great Domesday which had begun to make inroads on the parchment outer leaves of the text. The Little Domesday boards appear to have been less susceptible to attack. As soon as it was noticed the volumes were immediately rebound 'by a skilful person in the office, and it may be reported that both volumes are very handsomely and substantially bound in Russia leather'.[4] The 'skilful person', or possibly John Caley, retained the old boards, thus ensuring that six hundred years of binding history were not thrown away.

The 1819 bindings, which do not survive, were on flexible cords, probably with five hollow and imitation raised bands resembling the Abbreviatio (see colour plate D), a thirteenth-century manuscript, which was rebound at the same time[5]. In an effort to avoid the damaged areas of the spine the cords were grouped between the old sewing holes, but that merely lengthened the area which eventually needed conservation. However, the bindings were regarded by Sir Francis Palgrave as too tight.[6] The opportunity to remedy that came in the 1860s with the suggestion by Sir Henry James, director of the Ordnance Survey, that the document should be photographed and published in facsimile; public interest was considerable and the Master of the Rolls was in favour. One of Palgrave's last acts as Deputy Keeper before handing over to Thomas Duffus Hardy was to add his agreement, and

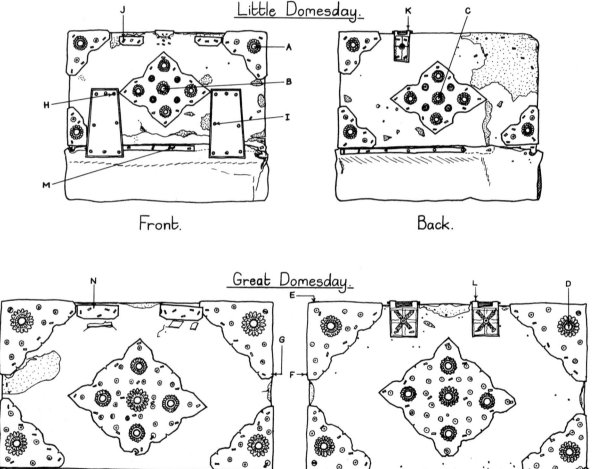

21 *Metalwork on 'Tudor' boards.*

28

22 *Sir Francis Palgrave.*

the Record Office binder, Hood, removed the initial section which was to be tried as an experiment. It was followed in turn by the other folios as the remainder of the text was photographed in Southampton. Once they were replaced in the Record Office in March 1864 argument raged over the best means of producing a binding appropriate to the place of the text in English history. Various designs were suggested, either jewelled or gilt, displaying an acute sense of history but a fine disregard for the working nature of the document. More attention was paid to whether the cover should contain symbolic historical representations than to the structure of the binding and the needs of the manuscript. Henry Cole, once an assistant keeper, now joint-secretary of the Department of Science and Art, at first favoured the ornate approach before re-thinking his position and opting for a simple solution. Eventually, after lengthy bureaucratic delays, the matter was taken out of the hands of

23 Little Domesday f.437v, 442r. Close up of Victorian repairer's name (J. Kew) in fold.

Cole and Hardy and given to the Stationery Office, which promptly reverted to the original idea of holding a competition for the best design. Nine months later Cole's first favourite, Robert Rivière, produced a design which was acceptable, and by November 1869 the volumes were completed.

The binding was done on double cords and was flexible. Evidence of the wear and tear on the joints and last gatherings caused Rivière to oversew them with silk. He, or his assistant, J Kew, whose signature occurs in the gutter of folios 437 and 442, also carried out a number of repairs to the spines. The repairs undertaken at that date are easily identified from earlier attempts at conservation by the heavy scarfing of both the repair parchment and the original. The covers were of black,

24   R. Riviere's bindings 1869. Great and Little Domesday.

stamped, leather on heavy card, the stamping being done from single blocks, incorporating the words Domesday Book on the front and back. The design includes Tudor roses, probably following the earlier metal design. The corners have heavy silver bosses, joined with a silver strip along the edges. More argument, this time with the Treasury, over the cost of the proposed cases for the display of the books still further delayed their return to the public gaze, but with some small savings they were at last adequately displayed, at a total cost of £125 10s and interminable delay.

It was in those boards that the volumes survived two world wars until 1952 when it was decided to rebind them in a more appropriate manner and to investigate the physical history of Domesday. Once they were broken down, it was found that the spines of the membranes needed urgent repair, where 'successive sewing holes have in some cases run together into long slits'.[7] The work was calculated at the time to add an inch or more to the thickness at the spine of Little Domesday, an addition which could not be avoided by backing. All the additional sheets which had been discarded by Rivière, apart from the end sheets of the 1819 binding, were included and the gatherings were sewn to meeting guards. Figure-of-eight sewing was then used on split leather bands laced into the oak boards. The back was quarter-bound with white tawed pigskin for Great Domesday and white tawed goatskin for the smaller volume. Despite the belief that a solution had been found for the problems involved in effective display of the volumes, events proved otherwise.

REFERENCES

1   *Domesday Rebound,* p.39.

2   E 403/193, m.10.

3   W Stubbs, (ed.), *Chronicles of the Reigns of Edward I and Edward II,* (Rolls Series) I, (1882), p.286.

4   PRO 36/7/224-5, 229-30, 237; T 1/1882/276.

5   E 36/284. The evidence comes from endpapers omitted in Rivière's binding, but on which the sewing holes are clear.

6   F Palgrave, *Kalendars and Inventories,* I, pp.lxiii-lxiv.

7   *Domesday Rebound,* p.40.

Conservation and rebinding 1984-1986

The chequered history of Domesday Book entered a new chapter in 1984 when it was decided to celebrate the 900th anniversary of the compilation with a major exhibition at the Public Record Office and the publication of a full colour facsimile of the text. It was clear that demand for facsimiles would increase with the publicity which the exhibition would attract, and that it would be further fuelled by the interest by schools in the BBC's twentieth century Domesday project. An elderly microfilm, taken by an amateur at the time of the 1952 rebinding and subsequently much used, was not of sufficient quality by contemporary standards to meet the projected demand. The production of a facsimile edition had the attraction of providing a security copy of the text and the quality would ensure the further decline in demands made on the original, a decline started after the publication of the first edition in 1783 and continued after the photozincographic edition appeared in 1864.[1] Such a copy could not be attempted, however, without breaking the two volumes down and flattening and conserving the membranes. The 1952 binding was too tight to allow effective photography.

Planning the operation had to take account of the requirements not only of conservation and the rebinding of the volumes, but also the needs of the various photographic processes to be used. The timetable for the work, which had to be completed in less than two years, had to include the provision of security accommodation at Kew, the establishment of a Domesday team and their separate workshop, and facilities for three different groups of photographers or microfilm teams. It had also to allow for the inevitable interest by the press, let alone conservators, binders, archivists and librarians from all over the world. The unknown factor was the length of time needed for the conservation work.

Once detailed investigation of the membranes began it became clear that considerable improvements could be effected to the previous repairs and to the binding of the volumes. Through no fault of their own the conservators who had worked on the repair and rebinding in the early 1950s had been obliged to use materials which were not of the quality available in the 1980s. The choice of parchment was limited then and the constraints on expenditure were considerable. Thirty years later the parchment had become rigid and inflexible, causing the structure to react unfavourably. The folios were not thrown up for satisfactory display, and the meeting guards caused the original folios to bend over. A build-up of glue from previous bindings had also collected within the gutters, increasing the resistance of the bi-folia to opening anywhere other than in the centre of the volumes. To make matters worse, the earlier wet spine repairs on the dry parchment had contracted on drying to impact the folds, causing distortion and wrinkling. Additional defects were clearly visible in the swell of the spine which added $3\frac{1}{2}''$ to the thickness of the original text block of Great Domesday and $4''$ to the thickness of the smaller volume. Use of the line of the spine of the animal for sewing, where the skin itself was thickest, and the accretions of glue and earlier repairs thus presented an insoluble problem for the control of the slippery, greasy and awkwardly shaped leaves. In addition the value of the weight of the oak boards used as covers was negated by the thickness of the meeting guards, which

25 *Great Domesday. 1952 meeting guards.*

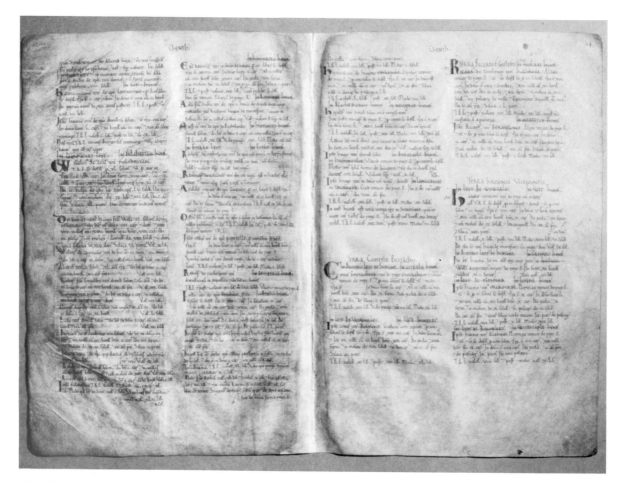

26 *Great Domesday. f.9v, 14r. Membrane badly creased.*

27 *1952 binding.*

prevented the boards from exerting a controlling weight on the parchment membranes.

Decisions about the location of the workshop and security precautions had to be taken in time to allow preparatory work before the main task of conservation and rebinding began. The modern building at Kew provided better facilities and was less open to disturbance than any of the other sites, and consequently two rooms within the conservation department there were adapted as a workshop and an adjacent photographic studio. Contiguity was essential, and the unit as a whole was separated from the rest of the conservation department by a specially constructed security cage. That provided a degree of isolation which both permitted the Domesday staff to work uninterrupted by distractions and also ensured that the two volumes, and in particular the loose membranes, enjoyed maximum security.

The workshop was fitted up with equipment and facilities for the three members of the Domesday team, who also had the use of a humidifying cabinet, essential for the controlled relaxation of the membranes. A twice-daily record of the temperature and relative humidity was kept, using a psychrometer, which allowed the environment to be monitored and checked: complete control was eventually achieved by introducing a portable humidifier which kept the room at a relative humidity of about 60%. The presence of even a few visitors was enough to upset the balance, but the problem was overcome by the simple expedient of either opening or shutting the door of the workshop. Such strict regulation permitted the conservators and binder to work on the parchment when it was flat and relatively immobile. Rigid adherence to the environmental conditions was finally to be matched

28　*General view of conservation workshop.*

by the provision of control within the case in which the volumes were to be displayed and stored. Only by adopting an overall approach which planned the operation from beginning to end could the value of the conservation and rebinding work be maintained.[2]

In addition to the obvious security measures taken to separate the Domesday workshop from the rest of the conservation department, care had to be taken to record the progress of each membrane as it went, in turn, from conservator to photographer, to microfilmer, and finally to binder. A strafo-plan board, with a coloured flag to represent each bi-folium, enabled the exact location of any part of Domesday to be represented diagramatically.

The materials used for the conservation of the volumes were chosen to provide maximum flexibility: the parchment was selected by the suppliers and lightly toned to avoid too great a contrast with the original skins. During its preparation in the department it was buffed still further and pared down to provide the minimum thickness consonant with adequate strength. In the places where the text prevented the use of parchment a transparent collagen was used.[3] Prepared from the air bladder of a fish, it has proved a more compatible material than the traditional silk for the repair of weakened areas of text. The adhesive chosen was wheat-flour paste rather than starch paste, a choice again dictated by the need for maximum flexibility. The majority of the parchment repairs were to be made on the spines and starch-pasted repairs are liable to crack and split if folded. Gelatine adhesive was rejected because it was too wet: evidence of cockled parchment from earlier repairs demonstrated the danger of using too

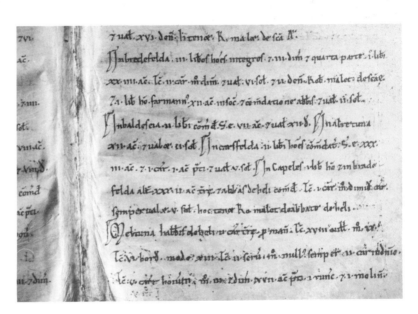

*29 Little Domesday, f.36r.
'Goldbeaters' skin on scored lines of
text.*

*30 Little Domesday, f.387r.
Centrefold distortion of parchment
by excess moisture.*

much water. The wheat-flour paste was accordingly made up in the workshop as needed and buffered to a neutral pH with magnesium hydroxide. It was decided not to add fungicide, to avoid the risk of chemical cross linking, but consequently additional care had to be taken to provide adequate air circulation when the volumes were finally placed in the display case.

The materials used for binding the repaired and flattened membranes were also traditional: given that there is no certainty about the initial covering materials, it was considered appropriate to use materials which were used on contemporary twelfth-century volumes and to continue the tradition started in 1952. Quarter-cut well-seasoned oak boards, selected fifteen months before they were due to be used, were dried, cushion-bevelled, and rebated according to

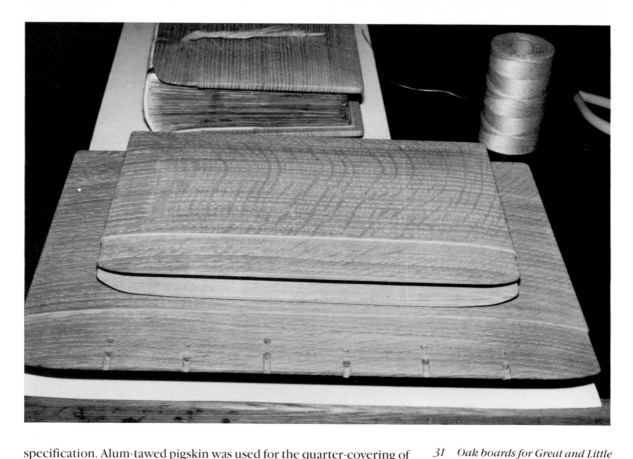

31   Oak boards for Great and Little Domesday, 1986.

specification. Alum-tawed pigskin was used for the quarter-covering of the spines and also for the loose carrying cases. For the structure of the bindings, unbleached hand-twisted linen thread (thrum) was used for the cords and the text-block was sewn with unbleached linen seaming thread (thrum 2A) which was waxed in the workshop. The choice was dictated by the need for flexibility and softness, to avoid adding to the swell at the spine. Flexibility and strength also dictated the use of cords instead of thongs: Domesday has been sewn on both during the course of its history. Bleached, waxed sewing cord was used for headbands. The boards were attached by lacing cords, wound from a thicker thrum, as were the headband cores. Wheat-flour paste was again used throughout.

The conservation work started in the autumn of 1984, after the sewings of Great Domesday had been cut, surrounded by a glare of publicity. Once that had been accomplished, each individual membrane was assessed and its condition noted. Full documentation of the state of each was important in order to decide on the scale of conservation needed: each flaw, oddity, unusual feature and previous repair was documented. Whilst it was accepted that the majority of the 1952 repairs would need replacement (although a few were retained as evidence of the history of the volumes), it was also clear that some of the earlier repairs needed to be reinforced. The scope of the work needed was limited, but the quantity was substantial. The condition of the membranes was basically good: there were no badly distorted or damaged areas, away from the spines, and there were no problems of blocked or fragmented parchment. The pagination had been established in 1952, following the numbering of the folios by Edward Fauconberge in the seventeenth century.[4]

Once the repair work began a routine was easily established. A total of four membranes a day proved to be the capacity of both the humidifying cabinet and the two conservators, and that was the norm established over the next nine months. Steady work at that pace enabled each membrane to be cleaned, relaxed, tensioned and conserved to a point at which it could be returned to light pressure, sufficient to keep the parchment flat.

Each membrane was systematically cleaned with an almost dry sponge and the 1952 repairs in the gutters were dampened with a sponge just sufficiently wet to release the adhesive and enable them to be removed. Once that had been achieved the old paste, glue and dirt from the fold area were removed, meticulous attention being paid to the remaining evidence of earlier bindings: no scraps of parchment, earlier sewings or apparently interesting pieces of evidence were removed unless loose, in which case the scraps were carefully retained against further investigation. Even dirt was removed only as far as was consonant with the required reduction in swell for the 1986 rebinding. The new repair parchment was then marked out on a light bench and, having been cut to shape, was further buffed down by hand, with a sandpaper block, and chamfered along the edges. Meanwhile the original membrane had been placed in the humidity cabinet, which was set to provide a moisture content of 95%. Most of the membranes were sufficiently pliable by the time their humidity had reached 22-24%: experience soon taught the conservators when the parchment, depending on its thickness, could be returned to the bench, placed on pressing paper, and tensioned with rexine-covered metal weights. Positioned initially on one side of the centre fold and then round the edges, the parchment was lightly eased into shape before the final weight was placed on the other side of the fold. Tensioning was thus minimised, the major concern being to flatten the originals, without altering their shape.[5] For that reason weights were chosen instead of

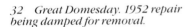

32   Great Domesday. 1952 repair being damped for removal.

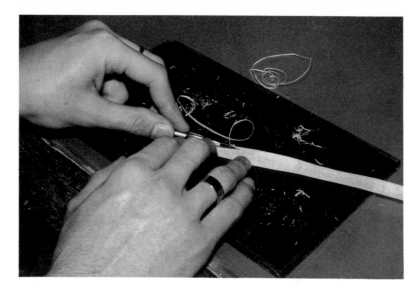

33 *Paring centre repair piece.*

34 *Placing membrane into humidity cabinet.*

clips. The pasted repair strip was then applied on a polythene carrier to prevent it rolling up. Once positioned, the polythene was removed and excess paste and air bubbles were flattened out with a bone folder. Finally the repair area was cleaned with an almost dry sponge.

The fish membrane (sometimes known as goldbeaters' skin) used for repairs over the text required different treatment. Initially it was washed in acetone to degrease it and then pounced with pumice powder, before being given an initial pasting while laid on terylene and allowed to dry. The uppermost side was marked for identification of the surface which would eventually be stuck to the membrane. Once cut to the required size the repair piece was laid on a wet black polythene strip and slightly damped on the pasted side. Black polythene was essential as the skin was so transparent that with clear polythene as a backing it was invisible. The repair was then applied to the text (the backing being kept in place), lightly rubbed down and finally flattened,

35 *Tensioning weights being placed into position.*

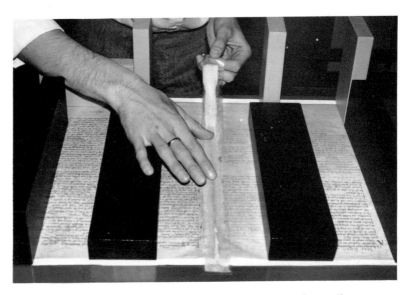

36 *Centre repair being placed into position.*

a needle being used to expel any air bubbles. An almost dry sponge completed any necessary cleaning. It was thus possible to avoid damping any areas of text beyond increasing the moisture content in the normal way in the humidifying cabinet.

When the membranes had dried out and any surplus repair material had been trimmed off, they were placed between pressing papers and put in a press under very light pressure until required by the photographers. Conservation work on the larger volume was completed by the middle of February 1985 and on the membranes of the smaller volume by mid July.

Installation of the Littlejohn camera for taking the plates of Great Domesday began in January 1985 and once the programme was running smoothly the camera men settled into a routine of completing shots of initially three and subsequently four membranes a day. A number of line and continuous-tone negatives were produced for each

37 Little Domesday. 'Goldbeaters' skin being applied to membrane at point of split.

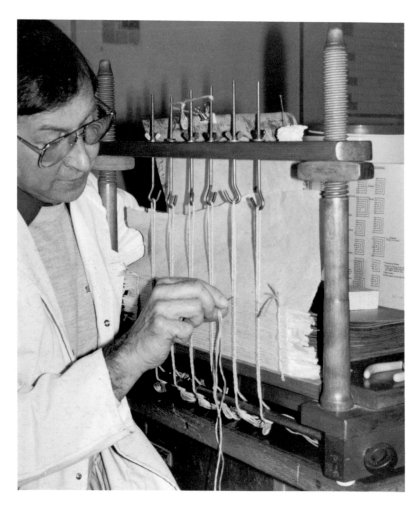

38 Concertina guard of paper and herring bone sewing.

sheet, from which four positives were made, each representing one of the printing colours. They were exposed onto screenless litho-printing plates from which the prints were produced. Of necessity the separate bi-folia were out of sequence for the process, since they were not re-arranged back into gatherings. Each membrane was placed between two sheets of glass to protect it against the change in the environment, photographed, turned, rephotographed and replaced in the press. The same procedure was carried out for Little Domesday but using a conventional copy camera to produce colour transparencies. The variation in technique was to accommodate the printing programme of the two volumes which was to be spread over some years. Microfilming the documents by members of the reprographic department of the Office followed the completion of the photography and the removal of the main camera. Much effort was put into the preparation and presentation of the membranes of both volumes. They were again filmed between sheets of glass, but this time sequentially, in order to provide a continuous film. Two microfilms were made, one a standard archival master from which working copies were taken, and the other a gold-treated archival master for conservation purposes. The latter has been stored, sealed in a surgical-quality stainless steel container, and pressurized by Argon to 1+ atmospheres, with a stainless steel film cord attached to the box to prevent any movement. The film container itself has been placed in a heat and fireproof security box, to remain undisturbed for an indefinite time.

Preparation for binding included making two dummy volumes to test the proposed methods and materials. The first trial volume was made to the original size of Little Domesday and incorporated a concertina guard of very thin hand-made Japanese paper to protect the spines from any possible contact with adhesive and also to give additional lateral strength to the binding. The paper proved more satisfactory than very thin parchment which was also tried, being more flexible as well as eaiser to control, and was subsequently used in the final binding. The control of the text block, however, was less successful. Criticism of the

39   Text block before sewing of part 2 of Great Domesday.

1952 binding had included comments on the difficulty of dealing adequately with such a weight of parchment in one volume and it was clear that from the point of view of conservation both volumes could be afforded much greater protection if they were further divided. Better control of the membranes meant less danger of the text becoming abraded by lateral movement, and the boards would exert a controlling weight on the parchment, keeping the membranes flat when the volumes were closed. In addition, more of the text could be displayed at once if required. Accordingly Great Domesday was split between Cambridgeshire and Huntingdonshire and Little Domesday was divided into the three counties it covers, Essex, Norfolk and Suffolk. The dummy of the large volume was constructed to test the effect of such a reduced text block and the method of sewing. It was also possible to appreciate the visual effect. The reduction in text block proved to be a satisfactory method of reducing the binding problems and the flexible sewing enabled the backing to throw up the leaves wherever the volume was opened. The twentieth century's two over-riding demands on Domesday were thus satisfied: preservation of the text and the ability to display the volumes to their best advantage.

Before the final stages of binding could begin the membranes were re-assembled into gatherings, the fold of each bi-folium being dampened very slightly and then bent over a thin board to prevent a sharp fold. Divided up into text blocks, they were then left under minimum pressure to gain their own equilibrium before the sewing began, in a constant relative humidity of 60%.

The sewing frame used both for the dummies and the originals was an adaptation of one lent by the Bodleian Library. The base was modified to allow easier access to the front edge of the sewing board and to the cords. The sewing was done on six double bands on the larger volumes and on four on the smaller ones: earlier bindings had a considerable variation in the number to avoid re-using weakened sewing holes in the spines of the membranes. Repairs over almost all these had made such considerations unnecessary, though in one or two instances the old holes were re-used where the parchment was suffi-

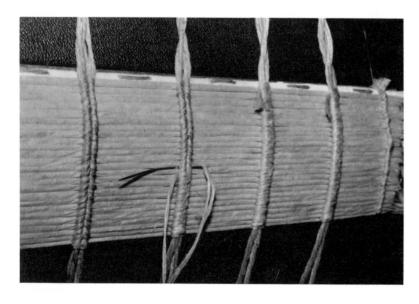

40   *Little Domesday. Pack sewing in the round on sewing frame.*

ciently strong. The sewing holes were pre-punched, using a larger diameter needle probe than the needle used in sewing the volumes, to prevent spiralling of the thread during the sewing process. The Japanese paper for the concertina guard was placed in position on the sewing frame and shaped with each gathering as it was sewn in. A piece of zinc was used as a former bent along one edge with a protusion of 5mm, which when laid against the cords enabled the paper to be folded over to form the zig-zag. A double thread, waxed just before being used, strengthened the herring-bone stitching. The kettle-stitch linking one gathering to another at the head and tail was reinforced with extra sewing thread to add strength to the head bands. While still on the frame the cords were slackened and the volumes were slightly rounded to facilitate the arching of the spine when open. The double cords were then pack-sewn to set the round. To protect the original text, now divided into five volumes and therefore partially unprotected, as well as the endleaves which were not part of the original but had been incorporated into the 1952 binding, a single folded bi-folium was added to the beginning and end of each volume with a pigskin leather joint and a linen liner tipped round and sewn to the volumes. The danger from weak organic acids from the oak boards was slight but it was advisable to take precautions. The headbands were constructed from a three-cord bleached linen thread, tightly twisted, which would not fray and was stronger than unbleached thread. It was sewn through the centre of each gathering under the kettle stitch with a bead front and back which held the headband firmly to the top of the text block. To prevent the danger of splitting the oak boards, the holes for the cords were staggered; drilling and channeling followed before the boards were drawn on to the text block and fixed through the two holes at each band position with wheat-flour paste. Pegging the holes, another potential cause of splits, was avoided by filling them with a mixture of paste and wood shavings or drillings which, when dry, were sanded down and caused no extra pressure. Between the bands a lining of alum-tawed pigskin was pasted into position and extended just over the joint of each text block for strength. A full lining of the same was added, worked to be as

41   Great Domesday. Head-bands partly sewn, back view.

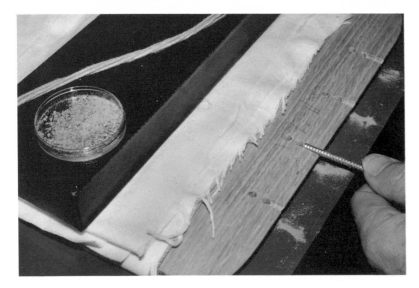

42   Little Domesday. Rebates between drill holes being filed.

43   Little Domesday. Cords drawn on.

flexible as possible, and the whole finally covered with a loose spine of alum-tawed pigskin joined only to the boards. When the skin was pasted down into the rebate the boards were lightly sanded and waxed.

For storage and to protect the outer binding, loose-fitting carrying cases were made from the same pigskins, (see colour plate E) and, once closed with foredge dowel rods, provided light restraint on the parchment. That is also provided by the lined boxes in which each volume will be kept when not on display. The dowels act both as carrying handles for the loose cases and as support for the spine when the volumes are on display. The immediate future for the newly re-bound volumes was as the centre pieces of the exhibition to commemorate the ninth centenary of the compilation of the text. Accordingly the volumes were kept in the same environment until installed in the specially constructed and conditioned exhibition case. Control over humidity was achieved by installing trays of Nikka pellets which had been previously conditioned to maintain the correct relative humidity. Replaced as necessary at intervals these provided a simple, non-mechanical solution for the purposes of the exhibition and subsequently for the more permanent display at the Public Record Office Museum. Storage of all the volumes together in one case, whether on display or not, means that they are all retained in the same conditions. Conserved, rebound, photographed, and microfilmed, and finally displayed in optimum conditions Domesday Book should remain the foremost English public record for at least another nine hundred years.

REFERENCES

1   E M Hallam, *op. cit.,* p.150.

2   A Cains, 'Repair Treatments for Vellum Manuscripts', *Paper Conservator* 7, 1982-1983, pp.15-23.

3   *Ibid.*

4   E M Hallam, 'Annotations in Domesday Book since 1100', A Williams, (ed.), *Domesday Middlesex,* (Alecto Historical Editions, 1986).

5   A Cains, *op. cit.*

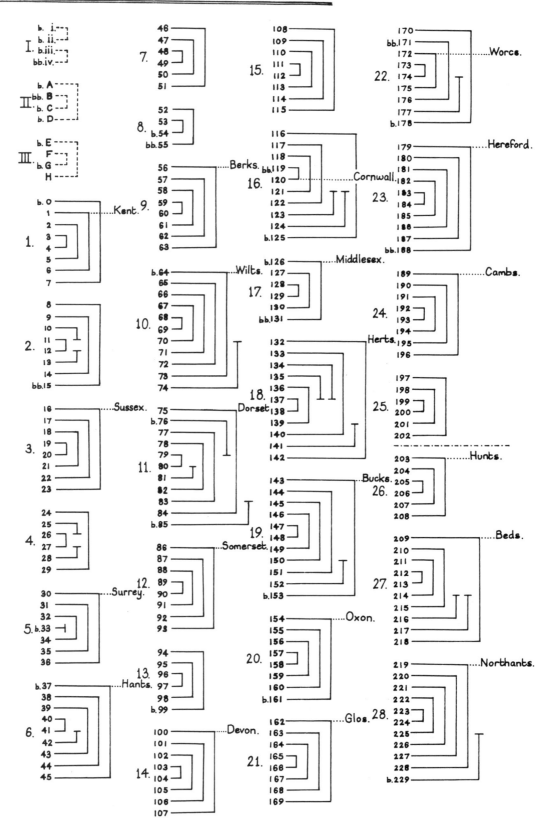

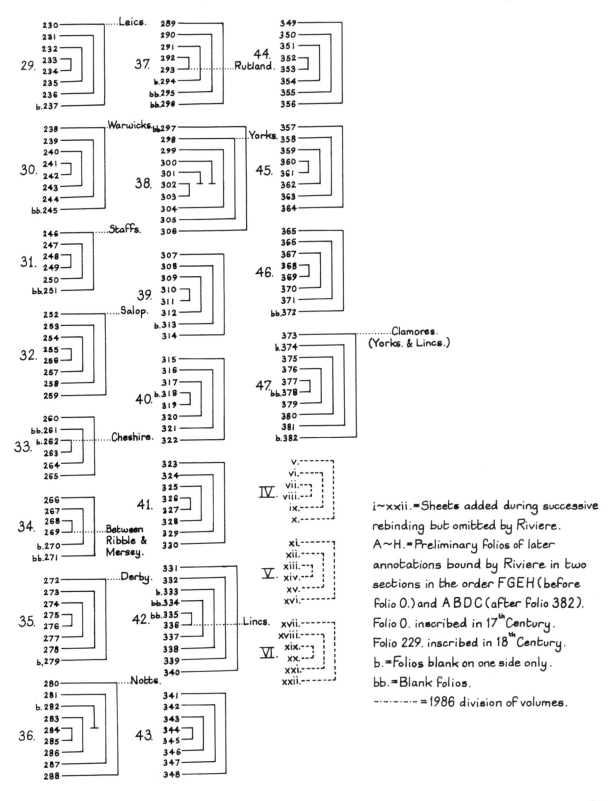

i~xxii.= Sheets added during successive rebinding but omitted by Riviere.

A~H.= Preliminary folios of later annotations bound by Riviere in two sections in the order FGEH (before folio 0.) and ABDC (after folio 382).

Folio 0. inscribed in 17th Century.

Folio 229. inscribed in 18th Century.

b.= Folios blank on one side only.

bb.= Blank folios.

–·–·–·–·–·–= 1986 division of volumes.

CHART SHOWING GATHERINGS OF LITTLE DOMESDAY.

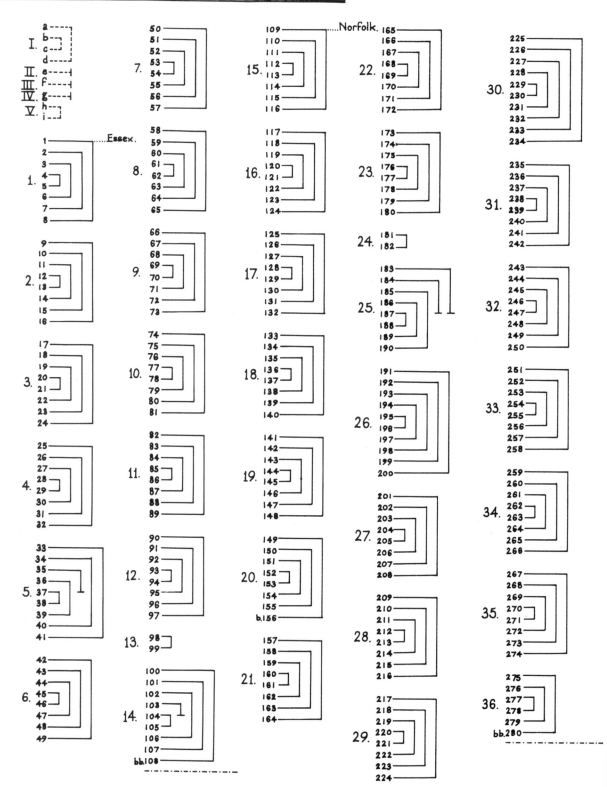

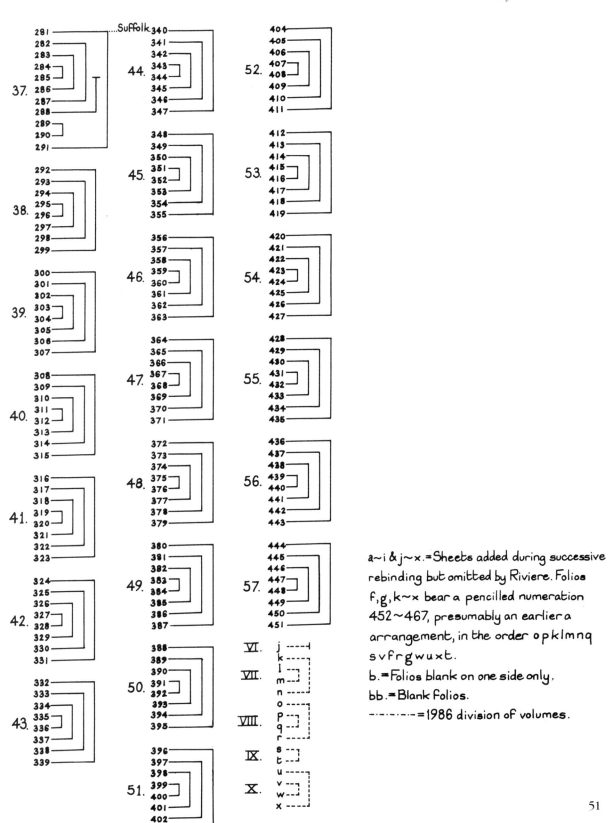

a~i & j~x.=Sheets added during successive rebinding but omitted by Riviere. Folios f,g,k~x bear a pencilled numeration 452~467, presumably an earlier arrangement, in the order o p k l m n q s v f r g w u x t.

b.=Folios blank on one side only.

bb.=Blank folios.

−·−·−·−·−=1986 division of volumes.

Timetable of conservation and repair work on Domesday Book 1984-1986

1984

2 July	Inspection of parchment by R Reed
3 September	Project begins. Equipment and repair materials ordered and prepared
21 September	Security cage completed
25 September	Great Domesday brought to Kew
27 September	Great Domesday dismantled
28 September	Numbering checked and irregularities listed
8 October	Stripping of 1952 repairs and replacement with more flexible parchment

1985

4 January	Littlejohn camera installed
25 January	Little Domesday brought to Kew
5 February	Photography of Great Domesday begins
13 February	Conservation work on Great Domesday completed
14 February	Initial examination of Little Domesday
28 March	Radio-carbon dating samples taken
20 May	Details of microfilming project settled
2 July	Camera for photography of Little Domesday installed
10 July	Conservation of Little Domesday completed
2 August	Microscopic ink samples taken for analysis by National Gallery
16 August	Photography of Little Domesday begins
6 September	Photography of Great Domesday completed
10 September	Palaeographical examination of text by Michael Gullick
14 September	Littlejohn camera removed by Westerham Press
16 September	Microfilm cameras installed
23 September	Microfilming of Great Domesday begins
27 September	Microfilming of Great Domesday completed
1 October	Microfilming of Little Domesday begins
8 October	Microfilming of Little Domesday completed
17 October	Microfilm cameras removed
25 October	Sewing of bindings begins

1986

15 January	Drilling of boards begins
4 March	Bindings completed

APPENDIX B

Domesday Radio-carbon Results

	Radio-carbon Years BP	Calibrated Years AD		
		Mean AD	68% confidence	95% confidence
Great Domesday				
OxA-660 Page	990 ± 60	1000-1020	980-1140	900-1205
OxA-661 Soft spine	550 ± 80	1330-1410	1300-1435	1285-1480
OxA-662 Brown outer	300 ± 80	1535-1630	1465-1660	1430-1805 1920*
OxA-663 Beech board	220 ± 70	1660	1630-1805 1535* 1940*	1485-1950
OxA-664 Page fragment	1160 ± 100	780-940	690-990	650-1145
Little Domesday				
OxA-665 Oak board	140 ± 70	890-940	775-980	690-1020
OxA-666 White goat	660 ± 60	1290-1375	1280-1390	1260-1410
OxA-667 Brown outer	480 ± 60	1430	1410-1450	1325-1495 1620*

*Indicates outlying values derived from calibration curve.

APPENDIX C

Metal types used in the Domesday book covers

Type 1) High purity, granulation technique 28-33% Zinc)

	Percentage of metal detected									
	Iron	Nickel	Copper	Zinc	Arsenic	Lead	Silver	Tin	Antimony	Area
Little Domesday										
Corner (boss)	0.45	tr	67.4	31.5	-	0.21	-	0.24	-	A
Central plate	-	-	66.8	32.5	0.21	0.20	-	0.31	-	B
Central (rev)	-	-	67.2	32.3	-	0.18	0.09	0.28	-	c
Great Domesday										
Corner (boss)	-	-	67.1	32.3	-	0.18	-	0.24	0.16	D
Corner (edge)	-	-	67.8	31.1	-	0.26	-	-	0.10	E
Corner (edge)	-	-	67.5	32.5	-	-	-	-	-	F
Corner (edge)	-	-	67.2	32.5	-	0.18	-	-	0.13	G

Type 2) Lower purity, lower zinc content although still probably granulation technique

	Iron	Nickel	Copper	Zinc	Arsenic	Lead	Silver	Tin	Antimony	Area
Little Domesday										
Nail on repair	0.24	-	68.1	29.9	0.23	1.50	0.06	- `	-	H
Nail on repair	0.17	-	67.4	30.3	-	2.05	-	-	0.11	I
Nail on repair	-	-	70.1	27.2	0.21	1.33	0.11	0.24	-	J
Edge of repair	-	-	69.1	28.0	-	1.71	0.12	-	0.12	K
Great Domesday										
Edge of repair	tr	-	68.7	29.3	-	1.52	0.10	-	-	L

Type 3) High purity, some lead and over 33% zinc

	Iron	Nickel	Copper	Zinc	Arsenic	Lead	Silver	Tin	Antimony	Area
Little Domesday										
Strip	0.30	-	65.1	34.0	-	0.38	-	0.25	-	M
Great Domesday										
Repair	-	-	66.1	33.5	-	0.34	0.05	-	-	N

Index

References to plates and figures within the text are in italic type.

Abbreviatio *25, 28*
acetone 40
acid, organic 45
adhesive (see also paste, glue) 39, 43
– gelatine 36
Agarde, Arthur 3, 27
air circulation 37
Anglo Saxon Chronicle 1
Anjou 1
Antiquaries, Society of 5
Argon 43

BBC, Domesday project 33
backing 31
bands, raised 28
– split leather 31-2
bead 45
boards, oak 32-3, 35, 37, *38,* 44-5, *46, 46*
Bodleian library 44
Bodmin prison 6
bone folder 40
bosses, decorative, *see* Great Domesday and Little Domesday
boxes, storage 46
brass, granulation technique 27

Caley, John 5, 27
Cambridgeshire 44
camera, Littlejohn 41
carbon 15
cases, display 31, 37, 46, 47
– loose carrying 38, 46
census, Roman 1
Chester, inhabitants of 3
cinnabar 15
clips 40
Cnut, King of Denmark 1
Cole, Henry 29-30
Collagen, *see* goldbeater's skin
colophon, Little Domesday 3, 15-17, *24*
cords, flexible 28
– double 30
– 1986 38, 44
– bleached, waxed 38
– lacing 38
Cornwall 6

Department of Science and Art 29
Deputy Chamberlains 3, 27
dirt 39
d'Oilli, Henri 17, *18*

Domesday Book, compilation 1
    extracts 3, 5
    abbreviations 3
    antiquarian interest 3
    publication *4, 5,* 5, 33
    photozincographic copy *5, 6,* 28-9, 33
    display 6, 31, 47
    1886 celebration 6
    studies 6
    physical make-up 6, 31
    1986 celebration 6, 33, 46, 47
    colour photography 6, 33, 41, 43
    dummy volumes 43-4
    division 44
– bindings, 1819 5, 27-8, 31
    1869 6, 29-31, *31*
    original 16, *20,* 21
    Romanesque 16-17, *26,* 20, *21*
    'Tudor' *24,* 27, *28*
    1952 6, *21,* 31, 33, *35,* 37
    1986 *31,* 43-7
– Great, content 2
    folio size 9
    parchment *8, 9, 10,* 11, *12-15, 34*
    cropping *8, 9*
    gatherings 9, 11-12, 31, 44, *48-49*
    re-ruling *10*
    format 12, *12-13,* 14
    headings 14-15
    scribe 12, 16-17, *17*
    style of writing 16
    beech boards 5, 27
    bosses *24,* 27, *28,* 31, *53*
    repaired *14*
    deletion 15, *15*
    sewing *20,* 21, 31, 38, 44-45
    calf leather 27
    clasps 27, *28*
– Little, content 2-3
    format 12
    size of folios 9
    parchment *8, 9, 10,* 11, *37*
    scribes 12
    gatherings 9
    sewing *20,* 21, 31, 38, 44-45
    headings 14-15
    pin 16-17, *26, 22,* 27
    1320 repair 21, *22,* 27
    strap *22,* 27
    calf leather *22,* 27
    clasps 27, *28*
    17th century repair 27
    bosses 27, *28,* 31, *53*
Domesday chest *4*
Domesday inquisition 1
– returns to 2, 3

Eadwine psalter *23*
Eden river 1
Edward the Confessor 2
Edward II 21
endbands, earliest 21
endsheets (endleaves) 31, 45
Essex 3, 9, 16, 21, 44
Exchequer 2, 3

exemplars 16
Exon Domesday *2, 3*, 16

Farley, Abraham 5
Fauconberge, Edward 39
ferrous sulphate 15
France 1
fungicide 37

Galbraith V.H. 16
gall 15
gatherings 30, 31, 44-5, *48-51*
geld 1
– rolls 1
Gloucester 1
glue (see also adhesive, paste) 33, 39
goat-skin, white-tawed 32
Godmanchester, tenants of 3
goldbeater's skin (collagen) 36, *37*, 40, *42*
gum arabic 15
gutter 21, 30, 33

Hall, Hubert 6
Hardy, Thomas, Duffus 28, 29
headband 38, 45, *45*
hidage lists 1
Hood, – PRO binder 28, 29
humidifier, portable 35
humidifying cabinet 35, 39, *40*, 41
Huntingdonshire 44

Ink 14, 15

James, Sir Henry 6, 28
Japanese paper 43, 45
Jenkinson, Sir Hilary 6
joints 45
– wear on 30

Kettle stitch, earliest 21
– 1986 45
Kew, J. 30, *30*
knife 14

Lanfranc, Archbishop of Canterbury 16
lead 27, *53*
lead white 15
leather, brown calf 27
– 'Russia' 27
– stamped 30
light bench 39
lining 45
London 3, 6
Losinga, Robert 1

Magnesium hydroxide 37
Maitland, F.W. 6
Mantes 2, 16
Master of the Rolls 28
Meeting guards 31, 33, *34*
mercenaries 2
microfilm 33, 43

needle 41, 45
negatives 41
Nikka pellets 47
Norfolk 3, 9, 16, 21, 44
Norman conquest 2
'Norman yoke' 3
Normandy 1, 16

Ordnance Survey 6, 28

Pagination 39
Palgrave, Sir Francis 6, 28
parchment *8*, 9, *10, 11*, 11, 30, 36-9, *39*, 40-41, *40, 41*, 44, 46
paste (see also adhesive, glue) wheat flour 36-8, *40*, 45
– starch 36
pen 14
Peterborough chronicle 16
Philip I of France 2
photozincography *5*, 6, 28-9, 33
photography 6, 33, 35, 41, 43
pigskin, white tawed 32
– alum tawed 38, 46
– joint 45
polyptych 1
polythene 40
press 41
probe 45
Prüm, abbey of 1
psychrometer 35
Public Record Office, Chancery Lane 6
– Round Room 6
– Museum 6, 47
– exhibition 1986 33
– Kew 33, 35
– conservation dept. 35
– security accommodation 33, 35
– Domesday workshop 33, 35, *36*
– photographic studio 33, 35
– reprographic dept. 43
pumice powder 40

Radio-carbon dating 21, 27, *53*
Record Commission 6
Record Commissioners 5, 27
red lead 15
relative humidity control 35, 39
Rivière, Robert 30, *31*
Robert Curthose 2
rods, dowel 46
Rolls chapel 6
Round, J.H. 6
Royal Historical Society 6
rubrication 14, 15
ruling patterns 12-14, *12-13*

Samson, bishop of Worcester 16, 17, *18*
Saunders, William Basevi 6
scarfing 30
Scotland 1

sewing 38, *43*, 44-45
– figure of eight 31
– flexible 44
– herringbone *42*, 45
– pack *44*, 45
sewing frame 44, *44*, 45
sewing holes 28, 31, 44, 45
sheep 9
Shepton Mallet 6
silk 36
Southampton 6, 29
spine, lining 45
– loose 46
spine bands 21
sponge 39, 41
Stationery Office 30
Strafo-plan board 36
Suffolk 3, 9, 16, 21, 44
swell 31, 33, 39

Tees, river 1
temperature 35
terylene 40
thread, linen 38, 45
– waxed 45
tin 27, 53
Tories 3
Treasury 2, 31

Vexin, Normandy 2
vermilion (red mercuric sulphide) 15

Webb, Philip Carteret 5
weights 39, 41
Westminster 2
– Chapter-house *5*, 6, 27
Whigs 3
William I, orders inquisition 1
– goes to Normandy 2, 16
– death 2, 16
– reign 3
William II, accession 16
William le Bokbyndere 21
Winchester 2, 3
– scriptorium 3, 9, 16
World Wars I, II 6

zinc 27, 45, 53

56